A Country Woman's Christmas

Autographed with love for dear George and Juliet

By
Louisa Venable Kyle

Louisa Venable Kyle

Louisa Venable Kyle

Portrait by W.S. McIntosh

Copyright © 1993 by Louisa Venable Kyle.

All rights reserved. No parts of this book may be reproduced in any form without written permission from the author. Direct inquires to:
Four O'clock Farms
1422 N. Woodhouse Road
Virginia Beach, Virginia 23454

ISBN 0-927044-03-X

Printed in USA
Teagle & Little, Norfolk, VA

Photography by Taylor Lewis, Jr.

Acknowledgements

The essays contained in this volume were edited from the author's weekly columns which appeared in The Virginian-Pilot, a morning newspaper owned by Landmark Communications, Inc., during the years 1952 through 1958.

   The author thanks Mr. Frank Batten, chairman of the board of Landmark Communications, Inc., for granting permission to reprint the columns in this book.

Other Books By Louisa Venable Kyle
The History of Eastern Shore Chapel and
   Lynnhaven Parish
The Witch of Pungo
Ram Lam
My Virginia Childhood (limited edition)
A Country Woman's Scrapbook

Dedicated to my beloved husband,
Emmett Kyle
and my three daughters

Table of Contents

Introduction 8

Memories and Meanings 11

Bringing the Children to Bethlehem 47

The Tastes of Christmas Past 63

Epilogue 73

Introduction

Roses in December

There is a saying I have always loved: "God gave us memories so that we could have roses in December." Recollections from Christmases past return each year to delight us at this season. It is my wish to share with you in these pages my roses in December and to offer some ideas for "roses" of your own.

My memories are awakened by all five of my senses: the *sight* of a beautiful handmade ornament on a tree, the *sound* of a familiar carol, the *smell* of cedar and pine, the *taste* of plum pudding, and the magic *feel* of friendship. All these bring back to us the yuletides that we hold dear.

For those of us who have many years to look back upon, Christmas is a time of remembering. The first essay in this book describes the holidays I spent at my grandfather's house when I was a small child. For those of us who are young, it is a time to learn about Christmas and to fill the storehouse of the mind with enduring holiday events.

Christmas Should Be Seen.

There are many places to see it—busy sidewalks, lighted trees, toys in store windows and decorated homes. It should also be seen in the Christmas pageant, in the beauty of a starlit night, and in the woods, with the hopes of a white Christmas.

Christmas Should Be Heard.

There must be the sound of horns and bells and merry songs about jingle bells and red-nosed reindeer, all mingling with the joyous laughter of children. There must be familiar stories, and I have included in this book a few Christmas stories that I wrote especially for children. There must be the everlasting beauty of organ music in a church, the exaltation of "The Messiah," and the singing of carols together.

Christmas Should Be Smelled.

Fragrance quickly awakens memories, so the home should have its blend of special kitchen aromas—a mingling of roast turkey, fruitcake and fresh-baked cookies. There must be an abundance of evergreens, the fresh, clean scent of the out-of-doors, to give an ordinary room the hint of a forest.

Christmas Should Be Tasted.

One must store the memories of candy canes, a chocolate Santa Claus, popcorn, apples, star-shaped cookies and mince pie. At the end of this book are some of my family's favorite recipes. Hospitality in a glass of eggnog beside one's hearth with friends and family is a part of it all.

Christmas Must Be Felt.

There is the crisp cold of a sunny winter day, the warmth of an open fire, the hug about the neck by small arms, the feeling of trust in a small hand holding a larger hand. There should be within your heart the Christmas feeling that comes from giving rather than from receiving. Children must receive intangible gifts through experiences enjoyed with loved ones. And there should always be one special gift, if possible an unexpected one, that comes from the heart.

At this time of year we are lifted out of the commonplace and everyday routine into a finer climate. We pause in solitude to remember the shepherds on the quiet hills above Bethlehem, the wise men following a star, the Baby Jesus asleep in a manger. More important than anything we may do by ourselves is to keep the celebration of Christmas a family affair. In the very beginning, that's what it was—a holy family together in the lowly stable in Bethlehem.

Each new family should begin at once to build its own Christmas traditions, little customs to observe together year after year, some of which will carry over into other generations. At Edgewood, we have many such traditions. One of the most meaningful to us was begun long ago, when our children were very young. Before bedtime each Christmas Eve, after the children had hung their stockings and helped light the candles in the windows, we would all gather about the fireplace. No fire was burning, of course, because it had to be kept cool for Santa Claus to come down the chimney with ease. We would read "The Night Before Christmas" aloud together for the last time. Then, as we bowed our heads, the father of the family would offer a special Christmas prayer before the children scampered off upstairs.

This is just one example of the many traditions and customs that can become a part of a family's celebration of Christmas together. How you trim your tree, where the stockings are hung, where you build your Nativity scene and what you do for others—all these things form a pattern your family will follow through the years in keeping Christmas. Little intimate family circles become holy places on the birthday of the Christ Child, and it is well to remember that it isn't what we do for our children, but rather what we do with them at Christmas that leaves the lasting and cherished memories...the roses in December.

Memories and Meanings

Over the River and Through the Woods

Christmas in a small college community during the early 1900s is one of the happiest memories of my youth. For my father and his sister, who lived with us after the death of my mother, going home for Christmas meant returning to the large, rambling Victorian house where my grandfather and two maiden aunts resided. Since we spent most of the year in a narrow row house in the city, going to see Grandfather was quite an adventure.

Before the trip on the train, there was the excitement of packing trunks with mysterious packages and of the arrival of the "transfer man" with his horse and wagon to take our baggage to the station.

On the morning that we boarded the train, my brother and I got up in the dark. Along with us went several gallons of oysters in a wooden tub filled with ice. We never left without this contribution to the Christmas dinner at Grandfather's. The tub and its luscious cargo of oysters rode in the vestibule of one of the coaches of the train.

In those days, traveling 175 miles by railroad took most of the day. The local train stopped at every station, and everyone seemed to be on hand to greet it. Even business was suspended for the important arrival of the train. It was a sort of social hour. People coming home were welcomed, newcomers were given the once-over, and those departing were given a send-off. The train crew was ready with news about the weather and events up and down the line.

We made this journey so often that my brother and I could name all the stations in order. The wooden coaches in which we traveled were far from comfortable. Some were heated by stoves, and whenever the doors were opened, a cloud of coal dust and cinders blew in. We got a little dirtier as the hours passed, and at least one cinder had to be taken from an eye.

We always carried along several shoeboxes filled with lunch —

fried chicken, buttered biscuits, hard-boiled eggs and bananas. We ate constantly during the trip, for the railroad vendor (sometimes called "news butch") kept passing back and forth with his basket to tempt us. Who could resist the little glass replicas of engines and lanterns filled with small candies?

At the halfway point on the trip, my father would let us get off the train and stretch our legs. We went into the depot restaurant and were served large goblets of cold milk and slices of pound cake.

During the remainder of the trip, there were special things to see from the train window. When we saw the last of these, an alarmingly high trestlework on which the railway crossed a stream, we knew we had reached our destination.

The station where we left the train was always filled with people who knew my father as a hometown boy. We were met by a carriage drawn by two horses and were wrapped in warm blankets with heated bricks at our feet. Grandfather's house was only six or seven miles away, but in the winter, it took an hour to get there because the roads were deep in mud. By the time we reached the crest of the last hill and looked down upon the familiar old buildings of the college campus, it was late afternoon.

Grandfather was usually pacing up and down the veranda looking for us. He seemed very like Father Christmas himself, with his snow-white hair and beard. His wonderful laughter made him "shake like a bowl full of jelly." His pockets were always filled with pennies, and he never let anyone discipline us if he was nearby. How we adored him!

After the long journey, we were soon put to bed, first bathing in a small tub near the woodstove. The bedroom was lighted by a kerosene lamp, and there was a deep featherbed with bright red blankets and gay patchwork quilts. We went to sleep to the sound of the tin stove popping and cracking as it cooled.

The halls of the old house were freezing cold, and by morning, frost had covered the windowpanes. There was a skim of ice in the pitcher of water on the washstand in our room when we awoke, usually to find someone starting a fire in the stove. Soon, the little heater would be red-hot, and the water in the kettle on top of it would be boiling away.

Everything was different from our life in the city, and the days before Christmas were filled with interesting experiences. We played in the barn and went with the wagon to get more wood. If there was ice on the pond, we watched it being cut and stored in sawdust in the icehouse. We carried food to the enormous turkey gobbler that was being fattened for Christmas dinner; we watched hams being taken from the smokehouse; and we went into the cellar to get apples, which were polished and placed in a big bowl. Who can forget the smell of apples in a cold cellar? There was a constant and delicious fragrance from the baking in the kitchen.

Finally, Christmas Eve arrived, and we would borrow an aunt's long, black stocking to hang at the foot of our bed. The big cedar tree was still on the side porch. It was never decorated until we were safely in bed. Our dreams were of reindeer beating a tattoo on the red tin roof—the tapping of branches of an elm tree contributed to these dreams.

Excited as we were on Christmas morning, we had to stay in bed, opening our stockings, until the fire in the sitting room had been stirred up and the room made warm. Only then could we thrill to the sight of the enormous tree, set in a bay window of the high-ceilinged room, its tinsel and ornaments shining in the light from the kerosene lamps and its cornucopias filled with candy. Real candles were carefully lighted and allowed to burn for a few moments with a radiance that still shines in my memory.

We were hardly finished opening our toys when the hinges of the door to the pantry would squeak, and the servants and their children would tumble in. What excitement! The door to the closet under the stairs was unlocked, and from wooden tubs and crates and boxes would come candy, oranges and presents for everyone.

After breakfast, the men of the family went hunting, and we spent the morning visiting families that lived on the campus of the college.

The Christmas dinner was served at three o'clock. By then, all of the relatives had congregated, and as many as 20 people would gather about the large table. The old butler, who had been with the family for years, was assisted by two of his sons. The food was served quickly and efficiently.

Dinner started with large tureens of oyster stew. To the children, who were not partial to oyster stew, it seemed an eternity before the carving of the turkey was begun. With the turkey there was home-cured ham, rice, mashed potatoes, macaroni and cheese, baked tomatoes, salsify, spinach and eggs, parsnips, coleslaw, many varieties of homemade pickles, and rolls, corn muffins and biscuits. Everything was hot, of course. And no one ever thought of counting calories.

A friend of the family described the end of the meal this way: "Then came the desserts. From one end of the table, the eldest sister served plum pudding that came into the room burning with a blue flame. The hard sauce made it more delectable. At the other end of the table, the younger sister served ice cream, rich with the lavish use of cream and eggs, smooth as silk from long turning in a hand-freezer. The fruitcakes and coconut cakes and the other sweet things followed.

"At four or a little after," the friend recalled, "the guests who had gathered from far and wide went into the sitting room. The

animated conversation revived memories of a great and gracious past and stimulated thought in challenging discussion of current events. And always reluctantly, with mingled emotions of sadness that one of the year's most pleasant events had come to a close, and with thankfulness that one had been privileged to share in it, we would take our leave."

Some years ago, I closed the old house where these Christmas dinners of my childhood had been served. I brought away the large platters on which hams and turkeys had rested, the ironstone tureen that had held such quantities of oyster stew, and the tall glass compote from which gallons of ice cream had been served. They seem too large in my small house, and I know that they belong to an era of American entertaining that has passed.

The old house has by now been torn down, but I can remember it all and am glad that I grew up in an age when the world was at peace and when hospitality knew its finest hour. Those old-fashioned Christmases served as an inspiration for all the yuletides that followed.

Advent – the First Sign of the Season

Those who love Christmas keep it in their hearts all year long. But for many people, the Advent season—the four weeks before Christmas—marks the first serious preparations. Advent was first mentioned by Christians in 524 A.D. Many churches consider it the beginning of the Christian year.

Advent has been celebrated for centuries in Europe. When the early settlers came to America, they brought along and shared their Old-World traditions; thus, many of the customs we use today in observing Advent originated there.

From Scandinavia came the Advent wreath. It is used in many churches and has carried over into the home, where it has become part of the family's celebration of the season together. You make it four weeks before Christmas. It contains four candles, which are lighted in a simple ceremony with all family members present on the four Sundays of Advent. On the first Sunday, the youngest child lights the first candle after saying a prayer. The next week, the oldest child says a prayer while relighting the first candle, then lights a second one. On the third Sunday, which is called "joyful" Sunday, the mother of the family lights the two previously lighted candles, says a prayer and lights the third one. Finally, on the fourth Sunday, the father offers the prayer while lighting all the candles in their proper order.

Depending on the size of the family, the candle-lighting routine can be varied. Also, passages of Scriptures may be read instead of or along with offering prayers. More important than who does what is that the use of the Advent wreath become a family tradition for the enjoyment and fulfillment of all.

The Advent wreath can be used as a centerpiece throughout the yuletide season. There are many ways to make one, and size depends on where it will be displayed in the home. A circular piece of styrofoam, with four holes cut out for the candles, can be

covered with evergreens and decorated with bows attached to each of the candles. Or four candles in low candleholders can be placed about an arrangement of fruit on a round tray, and evergreens can be used to cover the candleholders and bare spots. The candles are often purple, since that is the color used in churches at this season, and sets of these can be obtained from church bookstores.

A variation of the Advent wreath is the Advent log. Children often make these in Sunday school classes to use in the home. Two Advent logs can be made from one small log, about six inches long and four to six inches in diameter, by sawing it in half lengthwise. The sawed, flat surface becomes the underside (so it won't roll away), and four holes are bored in the rounded top for the candles. It, too, is decorated with evergreens, and the same simple ceremony is followed for lighting the candles.

Another custom that delights small children during this season is counting the days before Christmas by using an Advent calendar, an idea that originated in Germany. The Advent calendar contains 24 small numbered windows, one for each of the 24 days before Christmas. Behind each window is a picture of a special facet of this season. On the night before Christmas, the largest window is opened, revealing the Madonna and Child.

The Advent season to me is the happiest time of the year. Amid all the hustle of my preparations—setting up our Nativity scene, choosing the Christmas tree, in the fragrant kitchen with my yuletide baking, and while addressing and mailing cards and wrapping packages—there are many times when the true spirit of the season creeps into my heart. As I grow older, I long to return to that childhood expectancy that once filled December. I can satisfy this longing best when I am close to little children.

During these weeks of Advent, I bring out my favorite Christmas books to decorate the house and share with my special young visitors. "A Bird's Christmas Carol" makes me weep every year, and Dickens' "A Christmas Carol" improves with each reading. There are many books about this season, but nothing takes the place of the old, old story found in the New Testament.

It is well to journey in fancy back through the years to the little town of Bethlehem where the miracle of the Christ Child's birth took place. Christmas giving brings us close to that stable in the Holy Land. It is when we remember the old and the lonely, those who are ill or poor, and those who though rich in many things need above all our love and care that we are able to place our gifts beside the manger and thus receive His blessing.

It takes much thought and planning to be ready to celebrate the birthday of Jesus, to prepare our hearts for it. And it is when we let the true spirit of this great festival of Christendom influence our lives that we keep Advent best.

Our Manger – A Happy and Holy Scene

The berries on my holly tree peep through my living room window. Beneath the branches of this tree is my bird feeder with a tile bearing the figure of St. Francis. It seems a fitting combination: the holly tree has long been associated with Christmas, and the beloved saint from Assisi gave to the world the idea of the Nativity scene as a way of interpreting the true meaning of Christmas.

It was in the year 1223 in a little church in the village of Greccio, Italy, that St. Francis built his first Nativity scene. He wanted to find a way to explain to the villagers, many of whom were unable to read, the real meaning of this holy time.

After obtaining permission from the Pope, St. Francis had a stable built in the church, placed a hand-carved figure of the Christ Child in a crude manger and brought in live animals to complete the scene. When his followers came to the midnight service on Christmas Eve, the gentle saint conducted the service by singing the Gospel story. The people were so filled with awe that they came again and again to kneel before the manger.

The idea started by St. Francis spread rapidly, and Nativity scenes have been a part of the religious celebration of the birth of the Christ Child for centuries. Throughout Europe, elaborate antique sets of statues representing the Holy Family, the shepherds and the wise men are in collections in museums and cathedrals. In France, the scene is called the creche, or cradle; in Germany, a krippe, or crib; and in Spain, the Nancimients, or Nativity scene.

The building of the Nativity scene in the home as a family tradition is a beautiful way of teaching small children the deeper meaning of this holy season. The figures may be ornate or simple, wood, carved or metal, dolls dressed in appropriate costumes, or inexpensive sets made of china, terra cotta or papier-mâche. The most unusual set I have seen was made from corn shucks at a mission in the mountains of Virginia.

In our family, we have always called our Nativity scene simply "the manger." But regardless of what it is called, the idea is forever the same—a little scene showing the first Christmas. It should be the focal point of the decorations in the home.

It takes many years to collect all the things that go into the completed scene, and it is especially important to keep all of the objects in scale. Each member of the family can contribute something as part of the setting, and children growing up should be allowed to buy some of the figures with their own money. The scene will mean more to them if they are given the opportunity to participate in the creation of it, and they will treat this special place in the home with a certain reverence. Often, in the weeks before Christmas, they will ask to say their prayers or have the Bible story read to them before the manger.

One of the joys of my manger is that I think of it throughout the year—perhaps when I find a tiny shell or a carved bit of driftwood washed up on an island beach, or a smooth stone in a distant land, or when I get a package through the mail that contains a small figure and is marked, "For your Manger." And after more than 60 years, I continued to search for and collect whatever will make my Nativity scene just a little more true, impressive and meaningful to all.

The best place for the Nativity scene is where it can be viewed by all the household. The top of a piano or bookcase or mantle are good locations. For many years, we built ours on top of the piano that was in the alcove in our living room, a space five feet wide and two feet deep. Later, after the piano had been removed, a large old cupboard took its place, and in it, with the shelves removed, the familiar scene is now built.

For the background of our scene, we use a navy blue denim on which small gold stars are pasted for the sky. Dark blue poster paper can be substituted for the denim. The hillside is made of pillows and boxes covered in some dark green velvet that was once a friend's evening dress. The desert and road are fashioned from rough burlap bags in which grass seed had been delivered. The stable was made by my husband from a wooden cranberry box, with a hole cut in the top for a small bulb that lights the interior. It contains dried grass, and its sloping roof is covered in Spanish moss. A lichen-covered branch is firmly anchored and becomes a tree overhanging the stable, and a small mirror becomes a pond. New young cedar trees are gathered from the borders in my garden and placed in bottles of water with a tablespoon of sugar added to keep them fresh. A courtyard is built from a large, flat tray of sand, and it is surrounded by rocks that were brought from the mountains for this purpose.

It takes several hours to build the background, and when it is complete and the little light on the top of the stable is turned on, the children gather around. My children are all grown up now and scattered, and my grandchildren live too far away to help. But we have no trouble finding a small neighbor or two to come and unpack the figures and arrange them about the stable.

When they arrive, the children find the basket that contains the mysterious packages awaiting them in the middle of the living room. Candles are burning, and the beloved carols are playing softly in the background. As they unwrap the packages, one by one, Christmas stories are told, and we delight in the wonder in their small faces as they gaze upon and hold the figures of Mary, Joseph and the Christ Child, along with all the shepherds, wise men and animals. They can hardly contain their enthusiasm as they carry out our directions for placement. But these directions, often as not, are unnecessary. Children seem to know instinctively where each figure belongs in the scene.

When all the characters have been put into place and everyone declares that "the manger is prettier than it has ever been"—and it always is—we share "Star of Bethlehem" cookies before the children take their leave. And with this simple ceremony down through the years, the house at Edgewood has been truly blessed for the Christmas season.

Many memories about the children who have been with us at Christmas time come back to us when the manger has again been

built. From the very beginning, when my young daughters would buy a figure each year to add to our manger, gifts have come from every conceivable place to become a part of it. Our little Bethlehem now contains hundreds of figures, many of which have been given to us by some of the thousands of children and friends who have visited it over the years and who have looked long for a special object just the right size.

There is the very special angel given to us by a little girl, who said that "it is to always stand at the foot of the sleeping Christ Child." We place it there every year. There is the little dog given to us by a boy on account of Rachel Field's story, "All Through the Night," in which a small dog that crept into the stable on the first Christmas Eve gives its impressions of that holy night.

Our camels were brought back for us from the Holy Land, along with a camel bell which provides sound effects for the youngsters. Legend tells us that when all the animals heard the sound of the wise men's camel bells, they came out to see what was happening. We illustrate the tradition that the animals were peaceable on the night Jesus was born by including a wolf and some sheep, and a lion lying down with a lamb.

One visitor, noticing that our scene did not have a snake, did some careful research. Then, she made a clay figure and painted on it the markings of a bagoon viper—a snake native to the Holy Land. She sent it, along with a note saying, "I trust this will be a suitable serpent." Thus, "Suitable Serpent" got his name and joined the other figures.

One young visitor created a turtle out of a walnut shell; another made a drum for the drummer boy, and still another painted a white sheep black. A family of cats was donated by a friend who had had them since her early childhood. A piece of petrified wood is also a remnant from another friend's young years, and a featherweight piece of driftwood was a gift from the bay.

Many of the figures testify to the international flavor of our collection. From France came a Santa Claus pulling the Baby Jesus in his sleigh; from Switzerland, a goat; from Germany, a porcupine made out of a burr; and from China, a carved wolf and bear. The angels flying over the stable are from France and Italy, and four tiny mushrooms were brought back from England by a grandson when he was a student at Oxford. There is a stone from Central America, which I brought back from a trip to the Mayan ruins, and another came from Lake Geneva. Our colorful crab was found by young neighbors on the Avenue of the Americas in New York.

Many storybook characters are represented, too, including Peter Rabbit, who always has his home under the roots of a fir tree; Billy Goat Gruff, who is about to cross the bridge under which a troll is waiting; and Rudolph with all the reindeer. I first painted Rudolph's nose red with lipstick; then, to make it more permanent, I used red nail polish.

There is a quarter-inch ladybug, a tiny cricket and ducklings swimming on the mirror-pond—actually, they're "feeding" as only their tails and feet are visible. There are tiny mice, a vulture, a chicken, a turkey, an elephant and even a kangaroo. The list goes on and on and on.

We mustn't forget the figures about which I wrote the Christmas stories in this book. The "Gentle Stork" is found in the stable, where she plucked the feathers from her breast and placed them in the manger to make the bed soft for the Christ Child. "Little Star," the baby camel, is also in the stable, and not far away are Talmia, the little lame shepherd, and Sarah and Nathan, the innkeeper's children.

For the six weeks that our manger is in place—from the first Sunday in Advent through Epiphany—scores of visitors from far and wide come to see it. Children who knew it years ago return with their own children to hear the stories they have never forgotten. The living room table is always covered with Christmas books, and there are music boxes and angels and candy canes that all children enjoy.

The children are allowed to touch the figures and rearrange them, and they especially love to hold the figure of the Infant Jesus in their hands. One small and active little boy, instead of breaking the tiny object (as his mother was sure he would), leaned down and kissed the figure of the Christ Child before gently putting it back into place. The carols that small voices sing, the poems that bright-eyed little people recite, and the Christmas spirit that their loving awe brings to us add to our joy as their hosts. We feel about our young Christmas visitors as Charles Dickens did when he wrote of children:

I love these little people, and it is no slight thing when those who are so fresh from the hands of God love us.

Every home should have its little Bethlehem, and it should grow with the family. Family traditions and rituals that are established and continued from generation to generation become associated with those who take part in them. A new mode of behavior may change the celebration somewhat in each age, but preserving the tradition of a manger scene can be that link in the invisible chain of simple and intimate family happenings that influences the observance of Christmas in the future.

And so it is through the light of Christmas in the eyes of my young visitors as they view my manger that I receive my most precious gift of the yuletide season.

Living Trees, Living Symbols

The tree was a symbol of Christmas before German immigrants brought to our shores the custom of having a Christmas tree in the home. Years before, St. Wilfred cut down an oak that the Druids worshipped and found at its heart a young fir tree. Of it, he said:

This little tree, a young child of the forest, shall be your Holy tree tonight. It is the wood of peace, for your houses are built of fir. It is the sign of endless life, for its leaves are evergreen. See how it points toward heaven. Let this be called the tree of the Christ Child; gather about it, not in the wild woods but in your homes. There it shall be surrounded with the loving gifts and rites of kindness.

If you decide to buy a live tree to plant out-of-doors when the holiday season has passed, it is not too early to pick out your Christmas tree even before Advent is at hand. If you do not have a place to plant it in your own garden, it is a welcome gift to a churchyard or a hospital. It also makes a wonderful house warming present for a new neighbor who is faced with the sometimes overwhelming task of landscaping and planting a large, barren yard.

There is a wide variety of live trees from which to choose. Being partial to blue-green, I like the blue spruce and the deodora cedar, but fir trees, spruce, hemlock, balsam and even American Box can be used as well. Size is of the same importance as in choosing a cut tree. The tree will look much smaller in the row in the nursery than it will in the confines of your living room, so you should know beforehand the dimensions your room can accommodate. When you have made your final selection, have the nurseryman measure and label it for you.

Pick the tree up on the same day you plan to decorate it, and water it thoroughly as soon as you get it home. Then, before taking it inside, place it in a large tub or any large flatbottomed container that will keep it in a stable, upright position. The tree will be heavy with dirt about the roots, so you will want to have someone on hand to help you place it. First, wet an old bath towel, place the towel over the burlap that is about the roots, and then lift the tree into the container. Keep the towel damp during the entire time the tree is in the house, but don't let the tree stand in water.

In addition to the large live Christmas tree that we decorate in the traditional manner with garlands and all of our favorite ornaments, we sometimes have a special smaller tree, about three feet tall. This tree is decorated in accordance with an ancient Christmas tradition, and since we use real candles on it, it is lighted for only a short while on Christmas Eve. We keep a fire extinguisher close at hand.

On the top of this special little tree, there is a star with silver threads flowing down from it, to remind us of the divine light that came down from heaven. Clamped to the outer edges of the

branches are 33 white candles, to represent the years that Christ was to dwell among men. I found these candles in a craft store. They were made in Germany. They are about four inches tall, with clamps attached. Then, we tie real red roses to the branches, each in a tiny glass tube to keep them fresh. Why red roses on a Christmas tree? Because according to many legends, red roses bloomed throughout the world on that holy night so long ago when Christ was born.

After it is decorated, I place this special tree in an area of my living room where it can be viewed by all. On Christmas Eve, when family and friends gather about the manger after singing carols in the Boxwood Chapel in my garden, we light the candles briefly, and our hearts are gladdened by the beauty of the scene.

 Trimming Your Tree with Memories

It is a sentimental moment when I take out my Christmas tree ornaments each year. Some of them date back to the turn of the century and hung on trees I knew as a child. Many others were collected as my children were growing up. They evoke sweet memories of the trees which brightened our household during their young years. I cherish them all.

Especially dear to my heart are the handmade ornaments, and because of this, another Christmas tradition came into being at Edgewood. For many years now, I have fashioned needlepoint ornaments for my children and grandchildren to hang on their own trees. Not long after the New Year has begun, I decide on a single pattern—an angel, a snowman, a candy cane, or Santa Claus. I buy the needed supplies, and an old and very dear friend transfers the pattern onto the canvases for me. I keep my sewing bag close at hand throughout the year to ensure that I will have these new ornaments ready for the next Christmas. And as each grandchild comes of age and leaves his or her childhood home, their own ornaments accompany them to adorn the trees in their new homes.

Handmade ornaments have been ever-popular all over this country. The best example is the tree that was placed in the White House as the official Christmas tree in 1975 by Mrs. Gerald Ford, who was then First Lady. This tree was decorated entirely with handmade ornaments, including 3,000 that were provided by the Colonial Williamsburg Foundation from its Folk Art Collection. Many citizens participated in the effort.

The fashioning of handmade ornaments (and other handmade decorations, too) is a project in which the whole family can participate, whether it is popping corn to string, or making chains of bright-colored strips of paper, or painting pine cones gold and silver.

If you live close to the ocean, you can collect sea shells. They can be used as they are—all that is needed is a small length of thread with which to tie them to the branches of the tree. Ornaments made from souvenirs from travels can be used in the same manner, and these bring back memories year after year. Small

glass mirrors can be decorated with glitter; eggshells can be painted with any of the variety of mediums available in craft stores today; cranberries can be strung; and, with a bit of imagination, clothespins can be turned into reindeer and angels.

A book published by the Colonial Williamsburg Foundation in 1976, entitled "Christmas Decorations from Williamsburg's Folk Art Collection," contains many wonderful suggestions and examples of handmade Christmas tree ornaments and decorations. The book is illustrated and the directions and patterns are easy to follow.

This year, I'm not making all my needlepoint ornaments in the same pattern. I am doing them in fine needlepoint, and each contains a small group of different images. But the custom remains the same—one for each member of my family. And I feel blessed to have so many loved ones surround me to share this tradition with me.

A Madonna Set Apart

Christmas is a time to honor all mothers, especially those awaiting motherhood. Those who have "walked with Mary to the blessed eve" find a special meaning in this holy season.

In 1937, I spent Christmas Eve in a maternity ward at a hospital with a friend who had just had a baby. During the day, as I walked up and down the halls, I could see framed in the doorways many new mothers with babies in their arms. As darkness came, carolers sang about the hospital grounds, and in some windows, there was the glow of candles. It seemed to me that surely this was a holy place, and here, as in Bethlehem, "the hopes and fears of all the years are met in Thee tonight."

On the back of an envelope I wrote the following words for my friend, and they became a poem called "Madonna." These little verses have since found their way to many other mothers of Christmas babies.

> *Dear mother of a Christmas Child,*
> *It is of thee we say*
> *(As spoke the angel to Mary mild*
> *In Nazareth far away),*
> *"Blessed among women, Thou,"*
> *Upon this holy day.*
>
> *For to this world your baby comes*
> *When music fills the air;*
> *And silently God makes this gift,*
> *His answer to your prayer,*
> *As Peace on Earth and joy abound*
> *And love is everywhere.*
>
> *And through the years you'll always seem*
> *A Madonna set apart;*
> *Within the warm niche of your home*
> *A blessing you'll impart*
> *If you keep the love of the Christ Child*
> *Forever in your heart.*

Caroling in My Garden Shrine

The Boxwood Chapel in my garden has come to mean much to me, and most of all at Christmas. On those rare Christmas days when we have snow—when the 12 big somber boxwoods are frosted in white, and the bare branches of the dogwood trees look like white lace, and the altar cross of weathered cedar is etched in a fine powder—it is beautiful beyond words.

This out-of-doors chapel was not planned for any special season, nor did we think of it as a future shrine when we planted the small "tree box" bushes more than a half-century ago. But as the box bushes grew tall and wide, they cut off this part of the lawn into a quiet corner. It seemed the ideal place for a garden chapel. We built the altar between two of the box bushes by putting cedar posts in the ground and placing a heavy board on top of them. On top of the altar, we put the cedar cross which was fashioned for us by a neighbor. Tall pines form the background. In front of them, dogwood trees make a lovely white reredos in the spring.

Through the years, the chapel has been used often for special services, and many people have come to it for quiet meditation. It is clearly visible as we enter and leave the house, and it has blessed us all. But at no time do as many people gather here as on Christmas Eve, just as darkness comes to the garden.

When our children had married and moved away and there no longer were carolers in our house, we talked it over with our neighbors and decided that it would be a fine custom to get together to sing carols on Christmas Eve. Our out-of-doors chapel was chosen as the perfect place for the community to gather, and everyone was invited to bring their children and a candle. We decorated the altar with holly and candles, and thus began a tradition that has continued to grow for more than 30 years.

At that first Christmas Eve caroling, a neighbor who taught music in the area schools agreed to lead us in the singing of the well-loved carols. With lantern in hand, she has continued to do so through the many years that have followed. We also had music from a friend's violin that year to enrich our service. Perhaps 20 people assembled for our first caroling, and the numbers have

grown each year.

    I have many lovely memories from these times we have met together on Christmas Eve. One year, a large flock of birds decided to stop for the night in the shelter of the box bushes. As we began to sing, we awakened them, and their chirping added a very special music to our caroling. Another year, we looked up at the moon and knew that an American was circling it in a spaceship, flying our flag. We said a prayer for his safe return.

    During the war years, our neighbors who were in the armed services were uppermost in our thoughts. For many years, we said special prayers for one of our neighbors and his family. He was a Naval officer whose plane had been shot down, and we knew that he was a POW in Hanoi. We rejoiced when he returned, safe and sound, to join us again on Christmas Eve in our garden. He told us of Christmas Eves in his prison cell, when at five o'clock, he would always remember that back home we would be singing carols in the garden. It made him less lonely to think of his loved ones gathered together. No one will ever forget the benediction he said for us on his first Christmas Eve back home in our garden chapel.

    Rarely has it rained on Christmas Eve, but one year an awful storm came up. Those brave enough to come anyway were invited inside to sing. We were pleasantly surprised when a neighbor who

had been Santa Claus at a church pageant knocked on the door. He dashed through the house and kissed all the ladies and children who were there.

Each year, this Christmas Eve gathering becomes dearer to us all. As the years passed and more and more homes were built in our neighborhood, members of the civic league and garden club volunteered to help with the service. One of the men made candle stands with glass shades. He puts them up every year along the path from the garden gate to the house. So many neighbors and friends now attend this annual event that we have overflowed the chapel, and several hundred people holding lighted candles turn the garden into a fairyland.

Looking back to my own childhood and remembering real candles burning on Christmas trees, we decided one year to revive this custom in our garden. Now, when we come to the last carol ("Silent Night"), we all put out the candles we are holding and gather around a large tree which is lighted with real candles. The sight of it becomes a lovely memory.

When the caroling ends, we open our house and all are invited in to see the manger. There are candy canes for the children and the chance for all to wish one another a "Merry Christmas." This time we spend together in the gathering dusk helps to bring the real spirit that lies at the heart of Christmas to friends, old and new.

A Candlelit Chapel in the Woods

Christmas in the country is especially charming if you can find a small chapel in the woods at which to attend Christmas service. There is such a chapel not far from my home. It was built during colonial times and restored in the early 1900s. It stands today quiet and serene—a symbol of the faith of our fathers.

Not long after the chapel was restored, the congregation began the tradition of an annual Christmas pageant, which continued through many years. The same costumes and properties were used over and over again, and several generations grew up to participate in the tableau as angels, Madonnas, shepherds and wise men. Those who go back each year to this lovely little chapel beside a country road on the Sunday afternoon before Christmas look forward to the occasion as a rare and inspiring privilege. No one can witness this simple portrayal of the Christmas story without being deeply moved.

As the shadows lengthen and the friends of the parish assemble, the sweet fragrances of pine, cedar and lighted candles mingle and fill the interior of the old building. Through the windows can be seen the winter woods, where evergreens stand out in splendor against the finely etched frames of bare branch and limb, and the brown fields, over which twilight casts a rosy glow. During the years when we have snow, the setting is beautiful beyond description.

Within the church, there is an air of hushed expectancy as the candles, in the windows and in the candelabra that fill the chancel, are lighted. No other light is used, and the candlelight enhances the loveliness of it all. Familiar Christmas music is played softly on the organ, and then the choir enters, holding candles and singing a hymn.

The narrator's voice comes from the pulpit, reading the words of Isaiah, "Comfort ye, comfort ye my people," and the service begins. As the Bible story is told, there are seven scenes to illustrate the age-old message. Between the tableaux, the choir and the congregation sing carols. The shepherds and wise men come up the aisle, and the other members of the cast enter through the pines that bank the chancel. The red curtains that hide the manger at last are drawn back, and there is the living picture of the beautiful Madonna looking down at the Christ Child; "Silent Night" is sung. Then the curtains close and there is the recessional.

When the pageant is over, the church empties, and we exchange friendly greetings under the starlit sky. The same stars that once looked down upon the hills near Bethlehem remain bright reminders that these are things that are eternal and unchangeable. Thus, peace comes to weary hearts and a troubled world at Christmas.

I wrote this poem about the pageant in this small chapel in the woods in 1958. It was later set to music and sung in the church.

> *Small ancient church, close to the woods,*
> *Each Christmas draws us nigh*
> *To kneel within your quiet walls*
> *And pray to God on high,*
> *While candles bright in fragrant pine*
> *Your chancel beautify.*
>
> *Sheltered within your sanctuary*
> *year after year we see*
> *In Holy Tableau portrayed*
> *The blessed Nativity,*
> *And listening in the winter dusk*
> *Hear carols' melody.*
>
> *Thus is fancy across the years*
> *Our pilgrimage we start*
> *To Bethlehem and Jesus' crib*
> *Where shepherds stood apart*
> *To bring to Him this humble gift*
> *The love within our hearts.*

Symbols and Customs

We have become so used to many of the symbols and customs of Christmas that we often forget that most have interesting origins or stories behind their association with this holy time. Mince, for instance, is symbolic of the spice brought to Bethlehem by one of the wise men as a gift for the Christ Child, so mince pies have long graced our tables at Christmas. They were once made only with latticed crusts to represent the slats of the manger.

The fact that the wise men followed a star in the East bring the

star into Christmas song and story. There has been much speculation as to what the Star of Bethlehem really was. Some students of the heavens have declared it a comet; others say a conjunction of several planets caused the brilliant light. Another theory is that it was the planet Venus, for Venus appears brightly in the East in the early morning every two years. When I see Venus just before sunrise during the Christmas season, I like to feel that I am watching the star that shone for the Three Kings.

Martin Luther is credited with having first placed candles on the Christmas tree to symbolize the Christmas star lighting the home. Candles on the tree were later replaced by electric colored lights, but candles remain an important part of our holiday decorations. Some sources say that Christians borrowed this idea from the great Jewish Festival of Lights.

The use of candy canes at Christmas originated in the Catholic church. It is said that priests offered them to young babies to keep them from crying during Christmas mass. They are shaped to look like a shepherd's staff to symbolize the shepherds "keeping watch over their flocks by night" on Christmas Eve. The white stripe stands for the purity of the Christ Child, and the red is for the blood He shed to save us from our sins.

Holly is the harbinger of Good Friday. When we use it at Christmas, we are reminded of the Easter season, for its stiff, glossy, sharp-pointed leaves and clusters of red berries represent the bush from which the crown of thorns was made.

The hanging of stockings before the fireplace on Christmas Eve follows one of the many versions of the story of St. Nicholas. There is a legend of a poor man who was unable to raise a proper dowry for his three daughters. Each night, the young girls would wash out their stockings and hang them by the fire before going to bed. They awakened one morning to find the oldest girl's stocking filled with gold. On the next two mornings, the same procedure was repeated for her sisters. Thus, hanging stockings before the fireplace on Christmas Eve is a reminder of St. Nicholas, who came to be known as the spirit of Christmas because of his generosity to those in need.

History tells us that Saint Nicholas actually lived in the 4th century in Asia Minor, where he was the Bishop of Myra. He was the patron of children and was most kind to them, distributing candy and toys and other things that delighted their hearts. He had a white beard and, being a bishop, wore a red robe—both of which are copied by those who wish to imitate him at Christmas time. His feast is celebrated on December 6 in the Netherlands, where children place their wooden shoes in a row in front of the fire to receive his gifts. He is called by many names, such as Kris Kringle or Bonhomme Noel. He was accepted by the English when the Dutch settled New York, and our Santa Claus is an American distortion of the Dutch name, Sant Niklaas.

The symbols and customs of Christmas are many, but they all have one thing in common—they manifest the spirit of the season which we cherish in our hearts.

Tales of Toyland

In those delicious days just before Christmas when I was a child, I experienced many of the thrills that my grandchildren and great-grandchildren enjoy today. The Christmas light in children's eyes remains a "glimpse of paradise," and the passing of generations does not dim it.

I remember some three score and ten years ago appearing in pageants in angel costume, singing the carols, making presents for the family, going to see Santa Claus and the delights of shopping downtown. I remember helping my aunt prepare presents, warm clothing and baskets of food for a destitute family. We went in a carriage to a cold dark house, and there, for the first time, I

saw poverty at Christmas. Early in life I was taught that it is more blessed to give than to receive.

The toy departments in the downtown stores that I visited as a child are no more, but they remain vivid in my memory. I think the most beautiful one was on the third floor of one of the larger stores. After being shepherded past the china and cut glass, we entered the gilded cage of an elevator that was lifted by pulling ropes. When we reached the top in this exciting ride, we stepped into a fairyland of toys.

Such dolls do not exist today—dolls from Paris and Germany in exquisite clothes, dolls with beautiful china heads covered in real hair in curls, dolls with eyes that opened and shut, and "character dolls" that looked like newborn infants. These dolls were all sizes: some as large as the child who wanted them and some small enough to fit into a dollhouse. There were the china Kewpie dolls, very popular when I was young, and the Celluloid dolls that could be put into water without harm

The toy departments had all sizes of teddy bears and wooden Noah's arks filled with animals. But nothing equaled the sight of the Stieff circus, complete with tent and jointed animals. I wanted one of these all of my childhood but never seemed to get the point across. There were hobby horses that seemed alive, with real skin and glass eyes, sets of china dishes, and pianos, and iron fire engines, and penny banks that were mechanical. Children played the same games then as now: jackstraws, parcheesi, dominoes and checkers.

The Christmas tree ornaments were very beautiful, and there were yards of tinsel on the trees. I am sure there was one Santa Claus (at a larger store), instead of many, which confuses the young today. I remember the one who stood by the Salvation Army kettle on the street and rang a bell.

We lived so close to the shopping area when we were children that we went over to it alone. There was a Woodworth's five-and-ten-cent store where you could buy lots of things for a nickel and a dime. To be downtown on the nights before Christmas was very exciting. The street lights in those days were a series of arches that extended across the street, and riding a streetcar beneath them delighted me. I can still smell the horse-drawn popcorn wagon and hear the whistle of the peanut man who roasted hot chestnuts at the curb.

One of my earliest memories was a Christmas shopping spree. My brother and I went with Mammy and my mother to buy red coats with black velvet collars. When I was five, I also had a black beaver hat with a red ribbon on it to complete this outfit. Some months later, the hat met a sad end when it blew in the sea lion's pool on a Sunday afternoon at the city park.

As a child, I was taught to make Christmas presents for family and friends. I embroidered pincushions and bureau scarves. In the pre-Kleenex days, I cut circles of tissue paper and made them into balls for gentlemen to wipe their razors on. At art classes, I produced presents of hammered brass and burnt wood, made calendars with original pictures on them and modeled clay into candlesticks and paperweights.

Christmas shopping was never complete without a visit to the children's favorite stores. Mine was Tripples, and it filled the basement of a house. Here we could buy tops and candy for a penny, and the owner, who I now know was one of God's saints, never seemed to mind how long it took a child to decide how to spend the pennies.

The candy counter, with its tall glass jars of peppermint sticks, lime barrels, marshmallow bananas, butterscotch patties, licorice sticks, and small black licorice dolls, was a sheer delight to choose from. There were wooden boxes of large gingerbread cookies, some in the shape of horses, and dill pickles in a barrel. The toys were Japanese dolls, and flowers that opened in water, and firecrackers and sparklers, which were part of every Christmas. There were jacks and tops and hoops to roll and jumping ropes. I shall never forget the toys in that little shop.

Calling in the New Year

The modern celebration of New Year's Eve has taken the place of a delightful old custom: formal receptions—called "at homes"—on New Year's Day. Calling used to be the tradition on January 1, but the vogue for these visits declined somewhat at the turn of the century.

President George Washington established this custom as early as 1790, when New York City was the nation's capital. President Washington held a formal reception for local and foreign dignitaries. He expressed the hope that, whatever changes might take place in the manners and customs of that city, the observance of New Year's Day would never be abandoned. Perhaps out of deference to his wishes, this form of entertaining remained popular for many years throughout America, and it made New Year's Day a merry holiday indeed.

In the seaport town where I was born and spent my childhood, the last years of the 19th century were a golden era in social life. Beautiful mansions lined the old streets. In their large rooms, which had long windows, marble fireplaces and great gold-leaf mirrors, lavish entertainments were held. The names of the city's prominent families were listed as being at home on New Year's Day, and hostesses outdid themselves, providing refreshments to which even an epicure would bow.

The parties began early in the day and lasted until the last caller had outstayed his welcome. It was a man's day, for the ladies of the family remained at home to receive, and young girls were allowed to help serve. All the gentlemen of the town did the calling.

It was an important day for eligible bachelors, especially young Naval officers who would club together and hire a hack for the day. Men wore cutaways, striped trousers, Chesterfield coats and silk hats. My father's silk hat stayed for years in its satin-lined leather hatbox, a reminder of his early days when he was a young lawyer just arrived in the city to begin his practice. The ladies wore gowns with sweeping trains, tiny waists and elaborate

trimmings. Picture hats with ostrich plumes rested on their pompadoured heads. Fur muffs and stoles often had bunches of double Russian violets pinned to them. When darkness fell, they changed into formal evening dresses and wore long, white kid gloves.

The parlors were decorated with palms and American Beauty roses, with stems four feet or longer, in tall Delft jars. Lovely epergnes of fruit and bonbons graced the tables, and carnations and other hothouse flowers were loosely placed in "vaa-zes." The finest Haviland, Dresden, Limoges, Canton and other china was used. Silver punch bowls, cake dishes, candelabra and old silver services on tables covered with the best linens all signified the elegant living of that period.

The food that was served was beyond description. Fifty pound blocks of ice were hollowed out and placed on silver trays. These held raw oysters. There were spiced rounds of beef, baked ham, cold turkey, chicken salad, pickled oysters, hot rolls light as a feather, small hot biscuits that melted in your mouth, Tipsy cake, fruitcake, pound cake, other small pastries of every description, and coffee, tea and sherry. Well trained waiters anticipated every desire of the guests; the service was impeccable, as was the food.

In the room upstairs where the gentlemen put their coats and hats, there was always a table with a decanter of whiskey and a box of cigars, for there was no drinking or smoking in the presence of ladies at these New Year's receptions. Downstairs, there was well-flavored punch, eggnog as smooth as velvet, and syllabub. Behavior remained above reproach, and the young blades of that day must have had strong willpower as well as strong digestions.

Laughter filled the high-ceilinged rooms, and the young ladies were forever peeping through long lace curtains to see who would be the next caller. There was a cordial welcome, a bit of formal conversation with one's elders, some flirting on the side and, after a brief sojourn, fond farewells and a Happy New Year's wish.

There was but one note of sadness to this celebration. Within the homes where there had been a death in the family the members of the household sat together about their own fireplace. It was an age of long and deep mourning. Black was worn by all, long crepe veils were demanded, and men had black crepe armbands sewn to their sleeves. No bell would be rung at such a home. Instead, a card was quietly dropped in the small basket that had been hung at the door for this purpose. This was a symbol that the callers did not want to intrude on the privacy of the bereaved family. It also let those who were in mourning know that they had not been forgotten.

Meanwhile, the carriages and hacks bounced along cobbled streets to stop in front of other beautiful homes. Butlers, who had watched many of these callers grow from childhood to maturity, waited to open great doors and welcome those who were expected to call.

Epiphany – the Night of the Magi

The sixth of January is the day we set about dismantling and packing away the manger at Edgewood. We chose this day to mark the end of our celebration of the holiday season because it is the Twelfth Day of Christmas, known in the Christian church as Epiphany.

Also called Little Christmas, Old Christmas and Twelfth Night, Epiphany commemorates the visit of the wise men and the manifestation of Christ to the Gentiles. It was first mentioned in 194 A.D. as a feast of baptism. Before the days when people could read, the date of Easter was announced each year on Epiphany. It has been celebrated for centuries in many parts of the world, producing many interesting traditions and legends.

In Syria, Epiphany is celebrated by the blessing of the rivers and streams. Many people bathe in out-of-door pools and brooks there. They believe that the pure of heart receive special blessings and that their wishes come true. To the sinless, the water feels warm; to others, it remains icy cold.

Epiphany Eve in Syria is the wonder night of the year. Children do not receive gifts until then, when the Gentle Camel of Jesus brings them. When they go to bed, they leave gifts of wheat and water for the camel and lighted candles in their windows to guide him.

In other countries in Europe, such as Spain, presents for children are brought by the wise men on the eve of January 6. The children fill their shoes with straw for the animals who bear the Three Kings to the manger. In the morning, cakes, candies and gifts fill the shoes.

In France, a special cake is baked for Epiphany, containing a tiny china doll. The one who finds the charm is crowned king or queen for the day.

In England, Twelfth Night grew to be a court festival of games. The old English carol known to us today as "The Partridge in a Pear Tree" tells of the 12 days between Christmas and Epiphany.

The Bible tells little of the visit of the wise men, but perhaps no three figures in history have had more legends grow up around them. The Three Kings have been given names: the eldest, Melchoir, King of Arabia, brought gold; Caspar, King of Tarsus, represented in ancient paintings as a beardless youth, brought myrrh; and King Balthasar of Ethiopia brought frankincense from the land of spices.

On the eve of Epiphany in many European countries, the initials of the names of the wise men—CMB—are written over the door of the home to bless the house for the year.

Our Eastern shores practice an unusual Epiphany custom. On the Outer Banks of North Carolina near Hatteras, this day is called "Old Christmas." On the eve of January 6, "Old Buck," the mythical bull of the Carolina marshes, roams the beaches. Children dress up to form a replica of this strange folk animal. People beat drums and celebrate with oyster roasts and other parties.

But stranger than all of this is the climax, when the Outer Banks tradition—that the snow geese depart on the night preceding Epiphany—is borne out by the sight of great flocks of these magnificent birds taking to the sky. The same stars that guided the wise men of old light the way, as the geese beat their wings and head north.

As night falls at Edgewood on Epiphany, the packing of the manger is complete. Early blooming shrubs have taken the place of the poinsettias and evergreens in the house. The last vestiges of Christmas are gone from sight, but they are not gone from mind. Each year I have many new memories from the joyous season to add to my roses in December.

Old Friends

As I write these words in my country house, the world outside is deep in a lovely whiteness, as if some giant bag of down had been unloosed in heaven. The snowflakes drift and dance through the air and come down to deck my garden in white finery.

A fire burns brightly on the hearth, and I have been busy taking down the Nativity scene and carefully packing away the figures. The New Year lies ahead of me, nearly 12 full months of it. I have been taking mental stock and wondering what resolutions I shall make and try to keep. I must confess that the braided rug under the dining room table still lies unfinished; it is a leftover resolution. Aside from all the material things that I hope to accomplish, there are other, more important resolutions on my mind.

Time moves fast as we grow older. The days, weeks and months slip together, and things we want to do go undone.

We detect an ominous threat in the saying, "It is later than you think," and it troubles the conscience. I miss most the pleasant hours spent with childhood friends. As I go through my Christmas cards and reread notes from faraway places, I realize again that a letter can bridge time and space and warm the heart.

The words of the old round that I used to sing with my Girl Scout Troop make a good resolution:

Make new friends, but keep the old,
One is silver, the other gold.

Each year opens new vistas in friendship. Persons yet unknown may come to mean much to us. But life's best gift in the end is childhood friends: those who have come along with us from our youth, who know all about us, who overlook our human frailties and who stand by us through thick and thin. Though they may not see us for months or years, they take up the companionship where it left off and welcome us with open arms.

Modern living, with all of its timesaving devices, moves at such a tempo that it is hard to set aside a few hours for informal visiting minus the entertaining. Only in times of sorrow or crisis do we drop everything and rush to our friends and neighbors. If there is any balm in times of trouble, it is these reunions and the comfort they impart.

A few days ago, I drove into a familiar driveway at noontime, hoping to lunch with an old friend. To me, she will always be the little girl who used to live across the street, who wore the middie blouse and who cut out Lettie Lane paper dolls with me on a rainy day. I can remember how we used to bribe each other to come to play with the offer of half an apple and two sugar lumps. When we are together now, it is easy for over half a hundred years to slip away, for lines to disappear and for hair to lose its silver. Like magic, youth returns to us for a brief hour.

I found the usual ready welcome and plenty of lunch. We fixed trays and sat down in the cheerful kitchen. We agreed that perhaps the burden of elaborate entertaining was one of the things that kept people apart. In some instances, it was the cause of loneliness. She remarked, as I often have said when people take potluck at my house, "If I had known that you were coming to lunch, I would have spent most of the morning in the kitchen and this way is so much nicer." I quoted her my favorite maxim: "That which makes a perfect meal is who sits in the chairs rather than what goes on the plates."

Over lunch, we chatted away. We reported on the activities of our grown-up children. We reminisced again about girlhood experiences. We agreed on our likes and dislikes, planned a trip over old country roads in a few weeks, and laughed in pure pleasure at being together. On the bird feeder outside, grackles and a thrasher fought over their meal and made us forget the dreary winter weather.

The clock on the wall ticked the hours away. All too soon we had to go back to our busy tasks. We were thankful for the interlude of rich contentment that had forged another bright link in the chain of happy memories that only old friends can share.

Yes, I've thought of a good resolution, not only for me but for many others: just looking up old friends. Nothing pleases me more than to have an old companion or former neighbor return to Edgewood, especially one of those friends of my children who loved it here when they were young. Tea is ready each afternoon, and there is usually something to go with it, in addition to a warm welcome.

Bringing the Children to Bethlehem

Favorite stories should be part of every child's growing up. And Christmas seems to be a perfect time, when families gather to spend peaceful hours together. Familiar tales are enriching and entertaining. More importantly, they help young people understand the true meaning of this season.

These stories tell about some of the figures in the Nativity scene that we rebuild every year at Edgewood. I wrote these tales especially for children, but they may be of interest to others who sometimes feel like they never want to grow up.

The Gentle Stork

This is the story of a gentle mother stork who lived long ago in Germany.

Winter was coming. The wind rattled the leaves on the trees that stood on a rocky hill above the River Rhine. Two great white storks and their young were clinging to the branches near their nest. The time had come to start the long journey to Africa, where they would spend the winter in the jungle with the elephants and monkeys and gaily colored birds.

It had been a busy summer. First, the storks rebuilt their old nest, and the Gentle Stork lined it with soft white feathers from her breast. She then laid two green eggs, and she and her mate took turns sitting on them, keeping them warm. One day, the Gentle Stork heard sounds coming from inside the eggs. The little storks were pecking at the shells, getting ready to hatch. When the shells broke open, what funny looking babies they were! They had no feathers, but they had long, long legs and great red bills that snapped together to say that they were hungry.

The parent storks found it took a lot of mice, frogs, small fish and insects to feed the young birds. The Gentle Stork walked on her long legs beside the river, hunting for food for her babies. When she saw a frog or a fish, her long neck with its red bill would reach down and snap up the food. She also hunted in the tall meadow grass for mice and insects.

Each week, the little storks grew bigger. Soon, their parents taught them to fly, and then to hunt for their own food. Their feathers were light gray, and they were proud young birds, copying all that the big storks did.

Now, summer was over, and the days were short and the nights were cold. The time had come for the storks to fly away south from the winter. The young birds were going to make their first long flight. The Gentle Stork and her mate flapped their wings and soared into the air. The young storks flapped their wings and soared into the air, too. With their legs stretched out behind them, they all flew on and on and on across the sky. Far below them were the snow-capped mountains, the winding rivers and the green valleys. They flew over a great sea dotted with islands. Soon,

they were above a vast desert, across which moved a caravan of camels. Darkness was falling when the storks glided downward over rocky hills, where shepherds were gathering their flocks of sheep into the fold and lighting their campfires for the night.

The family of storks alighted in the town of Bethlehem, near a stable. There were many people and animals in the courtyard of the inn near the stable. It was the time of the year when people returned to Bethlehem to pay their taxes. The innkeeper had had a good day, and every room in the inn was filled. He busied himself, watering and feeding the animals in the stable and scattering grain for the chickens. He smiled when he saw the big white birds, for he knew that storks bring good luck to a household.

As he closed the door of the stable, the innkeeper heard the clip-clop of a donkey as it entered the courtyard. On the donkey's back was a young woman named Mary, and by her side walked her husband, Joseph.

"There is no room in the inn," said the innkeeper. "I am very sorry."

"We are weary with journeying, and my wife must have some place to rest and sleep," begged Joseph.

"Could you use the hay in my stable for a bed?" asked the innkeeper. He opened the stable door, and the animals awoke and made noises as Mary and Joseph gladly walked in to share their shelter.

The Gentle Stork watched from the windowsill as the chickens settled on their roosts and the cows lay down and chewed their cud. All was calm in the warm stable, and the moon shone between the cracks in the roof. The little town of Bethlehem, how still it lay.

Suddenly, a strange sound awakened the Gentle Stork. It was the cry of a newborn baby—the little Lord Jesus lay in his mother's arms. The Gentle Stork watched as Joseph filled the cows' manger with fresh hay. She understood that he was making a nest for the Baby. She walked slowly to the bed that Joseph had made, and with her bill, she plucked feathers from her breast and made the bed soft and white for the newborn Child. Thus, the Gentle Stork gave the very first Christmas gift.

As Joseph placed the Infant Jesus on the warm soft feathers, the Baby smiled and blessed the Gentle Stork. So since that very first Christmas morning, the stork has been the special friend of all babies.

The Gentle Stork and her family rested all night in the stable at Bethlehem. They opened their eyes and saw the shepherds when they came to worship the little Lord Jesus who lay on the soft white feathers and the hay in the manger. When the light from the sunrise came into the stable on the very first Christmas morning, the four storks walked out into the courtyard of the inn on their long legs. They stretched their wings. Then they flapped them and soared up into the sky. With their bills pointed towards the south, they flew on and on across the desert and the sea, until far below there were green jungles.

The bare breast of the Gentle Stork Mother felt the warm sun, and in her heart, she felt peace and joy, for she had given of herself for the little Lord Jesus on that first Christmas morning.

Author's Note:

Many legends have grown up about the birth of the Christ Child, but none is as lovely as the story of the part played by the gentle stork. These birds have long been associated with babies, sometimes held responsible for their delivery. To us, receiving a visit from the stork signals the arrival of a new baby.

There are many references to storks in the Bible. They make

the legend of the stork in the stable on the first Christmas Eve seem more authentic. In England, the legend of the gentle stork has been read at Christmas for generations. A little poem, which was found on the flyleaf of young King Edward VI's copy of the first "Book of Common Prayer," tells the legend in quaint Old English. Some credit the young prince's father, Henry VIII, with the verses, but this is hard to believe. Others say the verses were written in the 16th century and were found in a prayer book in Yorkshire.

In recent years, the verses were set to music as "The Storke Carol" by J. W. Clokey and the English composer Donald Swann.

"The Storke Carol"

The Stork she rose on Christmas Eve
And said unto her brood,
I now must fare to Bethlehem
To view the Son of God.

She gave to each his dole of meat,
She stowed them fairly in,
And fair she flew and fast she flew
And came to Bethlehem.

Now where is he of David's line?
She asked at house and hall.
He is not here, they spoke hardly
But in the manger stall.

She found him in the manger stall,
With that most holy maid;
The gentle stork she wept to see
The Lord so rudely laid.

Then from her panting breast she plucked
The feathers white and warm;
She strewed them in the manger bed
To keep the Lord from harm.

Now blessed be the gentle stork
Forever more, quoth He,
For that she saw my sad estate,
And showed me great pity.

Full welcome shall she ever be
In hamlet and in hall,
And hight henceforth the Blessed Bird
And friend of babies all.

A legend so lovely and touching makes a wonderful gift for new mothers, especially at Christmas. It inspired me to write this story.

The Innkeeper's Children

Once upon a time, nearly two thousand years ago, there lived a little girl named Sarah and her big brother, Nathan. The children's father owned an inn, far across the world in Bethlehem.

All day long, people had been coming into the courtyard of the inn, asking for a place to spend the night. Some had made long journeys back to Bethlehem where their families had once lived. Sarah and Nathan watched the strangers unload their donkeys and camels, then feed and water them. Fires burned, food was being cooked in large kettles, and the smell of supper filled the air. Long before nightfall, all the rooms in their father's large house had been filled with guests. It had been a very busy time for the family. When it was dark and everyone was well-fed and had settled down to rest, Sarah's mother and father and her brother, Nathan, climbed to the roof of the inn, which served as a porch. There, they had a talk together before they went to bed.

On the hills that surrounded the little town of Bethlehem were shepherds tending their flocks, and now and then the little girl heard the bleat of a lost lamb. Sarah had never seen the stars so bright. There was one star that looked so big and so close to the earth that she felt she could reach up and pick it out of the heavens. Nathan was so sleepy that he could hardly hold his eyes open. He had helped his father all day. He had cleaned out the stable and put fresh straw in the stalls where the animals would lie all night. He had gotten water from the town well for the brown cow and the oxen, and he had fed them from the boxes that were called mangers.

Suddenly, there was the sound of voices in the courtyard and a knock at the door.

"Who is there?" asked the innkeeper.

"It is I, Joseph of Nazareth, of the house of David, and my wife, Mary, and we have no place to spend the night. Will you help us?"

The children and their mother had followed the innkeeper down the stairs. Sarah could not take her eyes away from the face of the beautiful woman in the blue cloak and the white veil over her head.

"There is no room," said the children's father.

"But the stable is warm and I cleaned it," said Nathan.

"Would you like to spend the night in our stable?"

"Yes. Kind animals will watch over us all through this night," answered Mary. The children watched Joseph as he helped her down from the donkey's back. Then Nathan led the tired little animal away and gave it food and water. Mary and Joseph thanked them, and the children closed the stable door and bid the strangers from Nazareth, "Good night."

Sarah lay on the floor on a rug, for there were guests in the place where she usually slept. From a high window, she could see the stars. Long after her mother and father and Nathan were asleep, she kept thinking about the beautiful Mary, who was spending the night with the cows and other animals in the stable of the inn. Finally, her eyes closed in sleep, but dreams came to her, dreams of angels who came down out of the sky singing, "Glory to God in the highest, and on earth peace, good will toward men."

While everyone was asleep in the inn, shepherds crept across the courtyard and opened the stable door. But Sarah did not hear them, nor did she hear the cry of a small baby, for like most little girls, she slept very soundly.

The sun was high in the sky when she finally awoke. Nathan was calling to her to come and see what was in the cow's manger. Nathan was very excited, but like all brothers he kept teasing his sister and would not tell her what he had seen.

Sarah was so curious that she couldn't wait for her breakfast. Out of doors she ran, and her sandaled feet carried her across the stone courtyard, where visitors who had stayed all night in the inn were preparing to leave. Her little dog and cat ran after her to the stable door. Nathan held her hand and kept saying, "Be quiet, be quiet."

The two children crept inside and a shaft of sunlight came through a hole in the roof and lighted the cavelike stable. Sarah's eyes were wide with wonder, for there sat the gentle and beautiful Mary looking into the cow's manger. In it, the little girl saw the loveliest baby wrapped in swaddling clothes. Sarah and Nathan fell on their knees, and as they looked into the faces of the mother and child, they loved them both.

"What is the baby's name?" asked Sarah.

Joseph, who was standing nearby, answered, "His name is Jesus."

Sarah held out her arms, and Mary let her hold the precious newborn baby. How soft and sweet the little Jesus felt.

"May I keep Him?" asked Sarah.

Mary smiled and patted Sarah on the head as she answered, "We must take Him with us when we return to our home in Nazareth, little one, but this tiny baby belongs to you and to all the children of God. Never forget the Baby Jesus. Keep Him forever in your heart."

And Sarah and Nathan never forgot the little Lord Jesus lying in the manger in the stable of their father's inn.

Calmia, the Little Lame Shepherd Boy

And there were in the same country shepherds abiding in the fields, keeping watch over their flocks by night.

High on the hills about the little town of Bethlehem, these same

shepherds were gathered about their campfires to keep warm. Their sheep had already been gathered together and herded into the safety of the fold for the night. It was a still, cold winter night on the first Christmas Eve, nearly two thousand years ago. Talmia, the little lame shepherd boy, was asleep with the shaggy dog that guarded the flock curled up beside him.

The shepherds were Talmia's family, for they had found him

years before when they were looking for a lost sheep. A strange whimpering had drawn them to the tree beside the brook, and there they found a little boy, scarcely two years old, who was very sick. He was too young to tell them his name and where his family lived. The kind old shepherd Joel took him in his arms and nursed him, and before many days had passed, the child was well again. They decided to call him Talmia, which was a name used often for little boys in far-off Palestine.

As Talmia grew older, he loved his shepherd friends. Only one thing was wrong, and that was that he had never been able to walk or stand alone. As he saw other children playing, he wished that he, too, was like them and could run and climb trees. Always, when the flocks of sheep moved from place to place, Talmia was carried on the shoulders of the shepherds. The lambs and old dog were his pets, and when he played with the lambs, they would butt him gently and nuzzle him with their wooly heads.

All day, Talmia would lie on a rug in the warm sunshine near the sheepfold. During summer, he could see beautiful flowers, for in Palestine, all kinds of wildflowers blanket the hillsides. He would listen to Joel's stories about boys who had lived long ago. Most of all, he liked to hear about another shepherd boy, named David, who had killed a giant with a slingshot and a smooth pebble. Talmia also had a slingshot, and for hours he would practice shooting small stones.

When night came, Talmia slept out-of-doors under the stars. Joel would point out several groups of stars in the dark sky and tell him that they represented birds, animals, fish and people, and there were stories about them all. For some weeks, the shepherds had noticed a very bright star that rose in the east. It seemed so close to the earth that Talmia imagined that he could reach up and touch it. He listened to the shepherds as they talked about the new star in the heavens above Bethlehem.

On that holy night so long ago, as Talmia was sleeping, the watching shepherds saw the sky grow brighter. From afar off, there was a strange noise like the sound of rushing water, then the brooks ran full after a heavy rain. Suddenly, there was music in the air. "And, lo, the angel of the Lord came upon them, and the glory of the Lord shone round about them; and they were sore afraid." The shepherds fell on their knees and covered their faces. The hair on the dog's back stood up, but he could not bark. Talmia, the little lame shepherd, awoke from his dreams, and though he, too, was afraid, he was unable to cry out. Never had the sky and the hillside looked so beautiful before. Far below him was the little town of Bethlehem, and he could see its flat-roofed houses. The angel was standing quite close to the little boy and touched him gently and said:

> *Fear not; for behold I bring you good tidings of great joy, which shall be to all people. For unto you is born this day in the city of David a Savior, which is Christ the Lord. And this shall be a sign unto you; ye shall find the babe wrapped in swaddling clothes, lying in a manger.*

Talmia, the little lame shepherd boy, could not understand what these words meant, and he could not take his eyes away from the angel. His whole body began to feel strange, and he huddled on the ground, trembling all over. Then, the angel took him by his hand, and before he knew what had happened, he was standing on his feet.

> *And suddenly there was with the angel a multitude of the heavenly host praising God, and saying, Glory to God in the highest, and on earth peace, good will toward men.*

The heavenly music filled the boy with wonder. All at once, he realized that the beautiful angel was no longer beside him and that he was still standing alone. He moved one foot slowly, then the other, and he was walking with his arms outstretched and his beautiful face looking up into heaven. A miracle had happened on the hillside above Bethlehem— Talmia was no longer lame. It was a holy night indeed.

As the music in the sky died away, the brilliant light faded, and there was only the glow of the campfire. Lambs stirred, and the sheep which had been asleep rose to their feet. The shaggy dog ran about as if looking for the strange angel he had seen. The shepherds, huddled together, were still alarmed by the sights they had witnessed. Suddenly, they were aware that their beloved Talmia was walking alone for the first time. Old Joel tenderly gathered him in his arms, and tears of happiness fell from the old man's face as he said:

"You can walk, my little Talmia, the angel touched thee and thou hast been made a strong, well lad. Let us give thanks to God who has caused this wonderful thing to happen."

> *And it came to pass as the angels were gone away from them into the heaven, the shepherds said to one another, "Let us go even to Bethlehem and see this thing which is come to pass, which the Lord hath made known to us."*

Down from the hillsides came the shepherds, and in front of them, with Joel beside him, walked Talmia, a proud little boy on his new strong legs. In the houses in the little town of Bethlehem, all was quiet, for only the shepherds knew about the wonderful miracle that had happened. Far in the distance a cock crowed. The faint light from a crescent moon cast shadows on the courtyard of the inn. There was a stirring as the animals in the stable moved about. When the shepherds opened the doors, the dim light of a lantern shone on the cows and on the small gray donkey. With these beasts, "the shepherds found Mary and Joseph and the babe lying in a manger."

They fell upon their knees and worshipped the little Lord Jesus, asleep on the hay. As Talmia arose to his feet and stood straight and strong, Mary smiled at the beautiful shepherd boy and wondered if someday her newborn son would grow up to be like Talmia.

And when they had seen it they made known abroad the sayings which were told them concerning this child and all that heard it wondered at the things told them by the shepherds.

And on that very first Christmas day so long ago in all the hills around the little town of Bethlehem, there was no happier child than Talmia, who would no longer be called the poor little lame shepherd boy.

Little Star

The camels that carried the wise men, and the camel boys who took care of them, went slowly over the road that went up the hills and down to Bethlehem Town. They were all very tired, for they had followed the star for many days and nights and had come a long way since they had left their homes.

The youngest camel, which everyone called "Baby Camel," had kept his promise. When he had begged his mother to take him with her to Bethlehem Town, he had promised to be very good. He had not once said he was tired, or that he wanted to go home, or that he wished he had not come.

Baby Camel's legs had grown very long since he left home. He was almost half-grown. The little hump on his back stood up, and his feet did not seem so big, and his neck had stretched out quite a lot.

The camel boy named Abou said, "Baby Camel, you are big enough to help carry some of the gifts that the wise men are taking to the little new King who has been born in Bethlehem

Town." Abou tied a small bundle to his back, and Baby Camel walked very carefully and looked very proud. He would put his head back and look up in the sky, where he could see the big star that was showing the wise men the way to Bethlehem Town.

    The wise men who had seen the star and who were following it to find the Baby Jesus were really three kings. There was the king who was a black man, and the king who was a white man, and the king who was a yellow man—three wise and good kings who ruled all different kinds of people in the world. They were bringing gifts of gold, frankincense and myrrh to the little Lord Jesus.

Baby Camel was worried because he had no present, like those that were in the bags on the camels' backs, that he could take to the King of Kings, as the Baby Jesus was called. When the wise men and the camels and the camel boys who drove them stopped to rest, the smallest camel would lie down close beside his mother and tell her all about it. The mother camel kept all of his troubles in her heart and told him not to worry, because somehow, there would be a wonderful present for the camels to give to the Baby Jesus.

When they reached the hillside near Bethlehem Town, it was late at night. The star that the wise men had followed seemed to stand still and to burn brightly in the sky. There were many stars in the sky on that holy night, but the star that had led the wise men was the brightest of all. There were shepherds on the hillsides taking care of their flocks of sheep, and Baby Camel heard them tell about the angels who had come down from heaven on the first Christmas Eve, and how they had sung:

*Glory to God in the highest,
and on earth peace, good will toward men.*

Baby Camel listened as the shepherds told of the new baby they had found in the stable, lying in a manger. He wanted to hear all about Mary and Joseph, but Baby Camel was so sleepy that he could not keep his eyes open. He fell fast asleep while the wise men, the camel boys and the shepherds were talking.

When he awoke, he heard a strange sound. And in the rosy light of early morning, he saw his mother licking a tiny, little baby camel that could hardly stand on her new wobbly legs.

Mother Camel smiled when she saw that he was awake and said, "'You are no longer the baby camel and you are much too big to be called a baby anyhow. Now, I shall call you 'Big Star,' because you have been such a good camel and helped to carry the gifts for the wise men who have followed the big star up in the sky all these months."

"And what shall we call this new baby sister camel?" he asked Mother Camel.

"Well," said Mother Camel, giving the new baby camel another lick with her tongue, "we must just call her 'Little Star.'"

As the sun came up, the camels were loaded. When they were ready to go, Abou, the camel boy, led Little Star very slowly so she would not get tired as they went along the road to Bethlehem Town to find the inn and the stable. And when they got there, they saw the cows and the donkey, and Joseph and Mary, and the little Lord Jesus, lying in the manger.

The wise men knelt down and worshipped the little new King and gave Him the gifts they had brought. And even the camels had a present for the Baby Jesus—for Abou, the camel boy, gave the tiny baby camel to Joseph, who led Little Star up to the manger where Mary sat. The hands of the Baby Jesus waved when He saw what Joseph had for Him, and a smile that looked like the tiny line of the new moon in the sky crept across the beautiful face of the little Lord Jesus. He seemed to know and to understand that Little Star was newborn, too.

Author's Note:
Among my Christmas visitors one year was my neighbor, Patty Mansfield. She brought me a present to add to the animals in my Nativity scene: a small carved figure of a very young camel. "This," she said, "is a baby camel for your manger. It is a she, and her name is 'Little Star.'"

The Tastes of Christmas Past

Christmas foods are enjoyed twice. First when they're cooking or baking, as the aromas of plum pudding or spiced beef bring back a flood of happy memories. And second when they're being shared with family and friends. I always think of delicious desserts as the edible presents we give at this time of year.

Special foods at certain meals can become as popular and traditional as singing carols. The following recipes are a sampling of my favorites for the yuletide.

Spiced Beef

25-lb. round of beef
4 oz. saltpeter
1 qt. black molasses
1 cup salt
2 oz. ground cloves
2 oz. ground allspice
1 oz. ground nutmeg

Rub beef thoroughly with saltpeter, then a little salt, and place it in a tub or keg. Combine last five ingredients for marinade and pour over beef. Let stand in marinade for 21 days or longer, turning the beef over each day. Remove from tub or keg. Tie snugly in cloth cover and place in a pot with cold water. Boil for several hours until done. Leave it in the water until it becomes cold. Serve with bone removed, rubbing the saltpeter and other ingredients in the hole, or leave the bone in. (This recipe can be made in smaller amounts.)

Oyster Stuffing

3/4 cup butter
1 1/2 cups celery, finely chopped
3 tbsp. parsley, minced
2 tbsp. onions, finely chopped
1 loaf day-old bread, cubed
2 eggs, beaten
1 pt. raw oysters, chopped, with their liquor
1 tsp. salt
1/4 tsp. black pepper
Milk (optional)

Melt butter in saucepan. Add celery, parsley and onions and saute until tender (golden brown). Put bread cubes in large bowl or in top of roast pan and add beaten eggs, oysters, oyster liquor, sauteed vegetables, salt and pepper. Mix well. If too dry, add a small amount of milk. Stuff turkey loosely and bake leftover dressing in small pan.

Pickled Oysters

Place oysters and oyster liquor in a saucepan and cook until edges curl. Skim out oysters, reserving liquor, and drop into cold water. Wash oysters thoroughly with hands and then drain. In separate bowl, strain liquor and combine 1½ cups of it with vinegar, peppercorns, cloves, mace, pepper pod(s) and salt to taste. Simmer mixture 5 to 6 minutes and pour over the cleaned oysters.

2 qts. oysters, with their liquor
Cold water
1½ cups vinegar
12 whole peppercorns
Few blades mace
1-2 red pepper pods
Salt

Cranberry Conserve

Cook cranberries in water until skins pop. Drain. Add apple and orange pieces, raisins and sugar and simmer until mixture thickens, about 30 minutes, then add pecans. Put in sterilized jars and seal. Delicious with turkey or chicken.

1 lb. fresh cranberries (note weight on package)
1 cup water
2 cups apples, peeled and diced
1 unpeeled orange, chopped
1 cup golden raisins
3½ cups sugar
½ cup pecans, chopped

Candied Grapefruit Peel

Wash grapefruit and carefully remove all pulp. Cut peel into strips ¼-inch wide and place in pan with salt and enough water to cover. Boil 15 minutes. Pour off water, add fresh water and boil 20 minutes. Change water again and boil another 20 minutes. This removes the bitter taste. After the third boiling, drain and cover with 2½ cups sugar and 1 cup water. Boil mixture in a heavy bottomed pan until syrup has evaporated, then spread on crumpled brown paper. When cool enough to handle but not cold, roll in ½ cup sugar.

3 grapefruit peelings
1 tsp. salt
3 cups sugar
1 cup water

Old-Fashioned Plum Pudding with Hard Sauce

- 1 loaf bread, cubed and lightly toasted in oven
- 1 tsp. ground cinnamon
- 1 tsp. ground cloves
- 1 tsp. ground nutmeg
- ½ cup flour
- 1 cup citron, chopped
- 2 cups apples, peeled and chopped
- 2 cups raisins
- 1 cup pecans, chopped
- 1 cup beef suet, finely chopped
- 4 eggs
- 1 cup sugar
- 1 cup bourbon whiskey or brandy
- Boiling water

Mix spices and flour together, then add fruit and nuts and shake to coat. More flour may be added if needed. In separate bowl, beat eggs and add sugar, whiskey, toasted bread cubes and chopped suet. Mix well and add coated fruit and nuts. Fill pudding mold ¾ full, cover and place on a trivet in a large kettle. Add boiling water so that it comes halfway up the mold. Steam 3 hours, adding more water as needed. Serve warm with Hard Sauce. Note: Plum pudding can be made well in advance and reheated in the mold by steaming until warmed through.

Hard Sauce

- ½ cup butter
- 1 cup confectioners' sugar
- 1 tbsp. rum or brandy

Cream together butter and sugar. Add flavoring and chill. Serve cold with hot plum pudding.

My Favorite Eggnog

Beat egg whites until stiff, then add ½ cup sugar. In separate bowl, beat egg yolks, adding 1½ cups sugar and 1 cup bourbon or brandy. In third bowl, whip cream until firm (when it takes shape), being careful not to beat too long or it will curdle. To egg yolk mixture, add half-and-half or single cream, 1 cup bourbon or brandy and the dark rum. Fold in egg whites and whipped cream. Add milk, stirring well, and store in large-mouthed quart jars. Let stand 24 hours and stir again before serving. Add more milk as desired if it is too thick or too strong. This eggnog will keep for two weeks.

9 eggs, whites and yolks separated
2 cups sugar
1 pt. whipping cream
1 qt. half-and-half or single cream
1 pt. milk
2 cups bourbon, whiskey or brandy
1 cup dark rum

Bishop Brown's Apple Toddy

Fill centers of cored apples with sugar, then stick 7 to 8 cloves in each. Place apples in baking pan and bake at 350° until soft (about 20 to 30 minutes). Remove apples carefully and place in large crock.

Make a syrup of 1 cup sugar, 1 cup water, orange juice and grated rind; cook until sugar has completely dissolved. Pour over apples. Cool. Pour brandy into crock; cover with plastic wrap and let stand from 7 to 10 days.

Strain mixture through cheesecloth to separate pulp and liquid. Pour pulp through a coarse sieve to remove apple peel and cloves, and reserve to use as a topping for ice cream.

Dilute liquid with apple juice taste, if desired. Serve with crushed ice in punch bowl or chilled without dilution. Yield: about 4½ quarts.

24 large apples, cored (preferably Winesap)
Sugar
Whole cloves
1 cup water
Juice and grated rind of 4 oranges
1 gallon apple brandy
Apple juice (optional)

Syllabub

1 pint day-old cream
1 cup fresh milk
1 cup cider
1/2 tsp. vanilla
1/2 cup sugar
Nutmeg, grated

Chill ingredients and make shortly before you are ready to serve. Mix all ingredients in a bowl except cream, which should be beaten slightly. Add cream, sprinkle with nutmeg and serve in cups.

Sally White Cake

1 cup butter, softened
1 1/2 cups sugar
6 egg yolks
1 oz. bourbon
1 oz. sherry
1 pound candied citron
1/2 lb. blanched almonds
1 7-oz. can flaked coconut
2 cups all-purpose flour
1/2 tsp. ground nutmeg
1 tsp. ground mace
6 egg whites, stiffly beaten
Wine jelly (recipe follows)
Whipped cream

Cream butter and sugar until light and fluffy. Add egg yolks, bourbon and sherry; beat until light yellow.

Put citron, almonds and coconut in blender container and finely chop; stir into creamed mixture. Combine flour, nutmeg and mace; add to creamed mixture, beating well. Fold in egg whites.

Spoon batter into a lightly greased and floured 10-inch Bundt pan. Bake at 250° for 3 hours. Turn out on rack to cool. Serve slices with wine jelly; top with whipped cream.
Yield: one 10-inch cake.

Wine Jelly

Combine boiling water, lemon juice, lemon rind and cinnamon; simmer 5 minutes.

    Soften gelatin in cold water for 5 minutes; add softened gelatin and sugar to hot mixture, mixing well. Strain through cheesecloth. Cool. Stir in sherry and refrigerate. Yield: about 4 cups.

    Serve with whipped cream, sweetened with sugar and 1 tbsp. sherry, or with boiled custard (recipe on page 72).

2 2/3 cups boiling water
Juice and grated rind of 2 lemons
2 small sticks cinnamon
2 envelopes (2 tbsp.) unflavored gelatin
1/4 cup cold water
1 cup sugar
1 cup sherry

Lady Baltimore Cake with Seven-Minute Icing

In large bowl, combine softened butter, sugar and flavoring and beat until light and fluffy. Sift together flour, baking powder and salt three times and add to creamed mixture alternately with combined milk and water, beating after each addition. Beat egg whites in separate bowl and fold into cake batter. Pour into three 9-inch layer cake pans, lightly greased with butter, and bake at 350° about 25 minutes. Cool completely, then put layers together with fruit-and-nut filling and frost with remainder of plain seven-minute icing.

Yield: one 9-inch three-layer cake.

3 cups cake flour
3 tsp. baking powder
3/4 tsp. almond flavoring
3/4 cup butter, softened
2 cups confectioners' sugar
1/2 cup milk
1/2 cup water
6 egg whites

Seven-Minute Icing

3 egg whites, unbeaten
3 cups granulated sugar
2/3 cup water
1 tsp. cream of tartar
2 tsp. light corn syrup
1 tsp. vanilla
1 cup golden raisins
1/2 cup candied cherries
1 cup dried figs, chopped
1/2 cup blanched almonds, chopped
1/2 cup walnuts, chopped

Combine unbeaten egg whites, sugar, water, cream of tartar and corn syrup in top of double boiler and beat until well blended. Cook over rapidly boiling water, beating constantly (about seven minutes) until icing stands in peaks. Add vanilla. Divide icing in half, adding rest of ingredients to one half. Spread fruit-and-nut mixture between cake layers and frost top and sides of cake with the remaining plain icing.

Star of Bethlehem Cookies (Sugar Cookies)

1 1/4 cups sugar
3/4 cup butter, softened (do not substitute margarine)
1 egg
1 tsp. vanilla
1 tsp. grated lemon rind
3 cups all-purpose flour (sift before measuring)
1 egg white, mixed slightly with 1 tsp. water
Granulated sugar, colored if desired
Blanched almonds

Combine sugar and butter until thoroughly blended. Beat in egg yolk, vanilla and lemon rind. Gradually sift flour into mixture, beating it by hand with a wooden spoon. Set bowl of dough in refrigerator for several hours or overnight.

To roll out, place a round ball of dough between two sheets of waxed paper and roll thin. Cut into stars with star-shaped cooked cutter and brush with the egg white/water mixture. Sprinkle granulated sugar on each cookie, and put a blanched almond in the center. Bake at 350° for approximately 10 minutes.

Yield: about 80 cookies, 1 1/2 inches in diameter.

Hermits

Combine shortening, sugar and eggs; mix thoroughly. Stir in coffee. Combine dry ingredients; stir into shortening mixture. Add raisins and nuts and mix well. Chill dough.

    Drop dough by teaspoonfuls about 2 inches apart on lightly greased cookie sheets. Bake 400° for 8 to 10 minutes.
Yield: about 7½ dozen cookies.

1 cup shortening
2 cups brown sugar, firmly packed
2 eggs
½ cup cold coffee
3½ cups all-purpose flour
1 tsp. soda
1 tsp. salt
1 tsp. ground nutmeg
2½ cups seedless raisins
1¼ cups chopped nuts

Jumbles

Cream shortening and sugar until light and fluffy; add eggs and beat thoroughly. Stir in sour cream and vanilla. Combine dry ingredients; add to creamed mixture, mixing well. Stir in nuts. Chill dough.

    Drop dough by teaspoonfuls about 2 inches apart on greased cookie sheets. Bake at 375° about 10 minutes, until almost no imprint remains when touched lightly with finger.
Yield: about 5 dozen cookies.

½ cup soft shortening
1 cup brown sugar, firmly packed
½ cup sugar
2 eggs
1 cup commercial sour cream
1 tsp. vanilla extract
2¾ cups all-purpose flour
1 tsp. soda
1 tsp. salt
1 cup chopped nuts

Tipsy Cake

1 sponge or pound cake, cut in serving size pieces
Sherry wine
Blanched almonds
Boiled custard (recipe follows)
Whipped cream
Candied cherries

Moisten cake with small amount of sherry and stick blanched almonds in each piece. Spoon cold boiled custard over each serving and top with whipped cream and candied cherries. Note: For whipped cream, whip ½ pt. whipping cream and fold in 2 tbsp. powdered sugar and 1 tbsp. sherry wine.

Boiled Custard

½ cup sugar
1 tbsp. cornstarch
Pinch salt
4 egg yolks, slightly beaten
1 pt. half-and-half, scalded
¼ cup sherry

Mix together sugar, cornstarch and salt and add to slightly beaten egg yolks in top of double boiler. Stir in scalded half-and-half and place over hot simmering (but not boiling) water. Cook, stirring constantly, until custard begins to thicken or coats a silver spoon. Season with sherry wine. Allow to cool, then refrigerate until ready to serve.

Huguenot Torte

4 eggs
3 cups sugar
8 tbsp. baking powder
½ tsp. salt
2 cups pecans, chopped
2 cups tart cooking apples, peeled and chopped
2 tsp. vanilla

Beat eggs until lemon colored. Add other ingredients in order. Pour into two buttered baking pans, about 8 x 12. Bake at 325° about 45 minutes or until crusty and brown. Serve in squares, crusty side up, covered with whipped cream or ice cream. Yield: 16 servings.

Epilogue

Priceless Gifts

In the days that follow December 25th, one is often asked, "What did you get for Christmas?" Instantly, we name off on our fingers the things that money has bought. But we keep in our hearts those gifts of memories, our roses in December, that are beyond price and outlast time.

As I relive the memories that the weeks of the Christmas season have given to me, I find many intangible gifts to cherish. The beautiful Christmas cards, with messages penned on them from friends who are scattered to the four corners of the earth, unite me once again with those I love who are now absent from me.

I can see other kinds of Christmas cards—nature's contributions—from my windows here in the country. A rare and lovely snow turned every corner of my garden into a winter wonderland. Redbirds perched on a holly tree. Two fat gray squirrels posed for me one morning in the dogwood tree above the pool and feasted on the red dogwood berries. These were live Christmas cards I'll never forget.

The woods gave us our Christmas tree this year. We had time to go tree-hunting, and deep in the silent, empty forest near our home, we found our tree. As we dragged it home, we relived similar expeditions as children and were transported back to the Victorian parlors of our youth.

The sound of bells is another intangible gift, one that is not forgotten. As a child, I heard horse bells on cobbled streets. Today, bells still toll in the town—bells that call me to remember the poor, bells that sound the familiar carols, church bells that chime out and peal the joy of the season.

The fragrances and tastes of Christmas are two more of the gifts I cannot touch. I savor the memories of the many smells of cookies baking in my oven, the roasting turkey that fills the house with its wonderful aroma and makes the mouth water. There is the subtle incense of bayberry candles and the frosty cold of a starlit night with the scent of wood smoke from a neighbor's yuletide fire. All of these awaken memories of Christmases past.

Christmas has always been a time when I receive renewed faith in the miracle of Bethlehem. Silently, many times during this season, the real but intangible gift of faith that lies at the heart of

Christmas comes to me. I have found it in little children's faces filled with awe by the story of the Christ Child. I've found it in the quiet of the crisp, clear winter nights in my own garden. The true meaning of that Silent Night so long ago comes most vividly to me in the service on Christmas Eve in my little garden chapel. Life is so generous a giver.

As I count the intangible gifts I have received for Christmas, I add one more: opening my door to find old friends ready with a handclasp, an embrace, and a greeting— "God Bless You and a Merry Christmas."

I cannot close my list of roses in December without adding the love of my family that I feel so keenly at this season. As the family circle continues to widen, making room for new members, I light the hearth fire remembering an old verse:

> *That home is where we love,*
> *Our footsteps leave but not our hearts,*
> *The chain lengthens but it never parts.*